PIE FROM THE SKY

HARSH HARLALKA

INDIA • SINGAPORE • MALAYSIA

ISBN 979-8-88749-834-8

For Maa, Paa and Sam

Contents

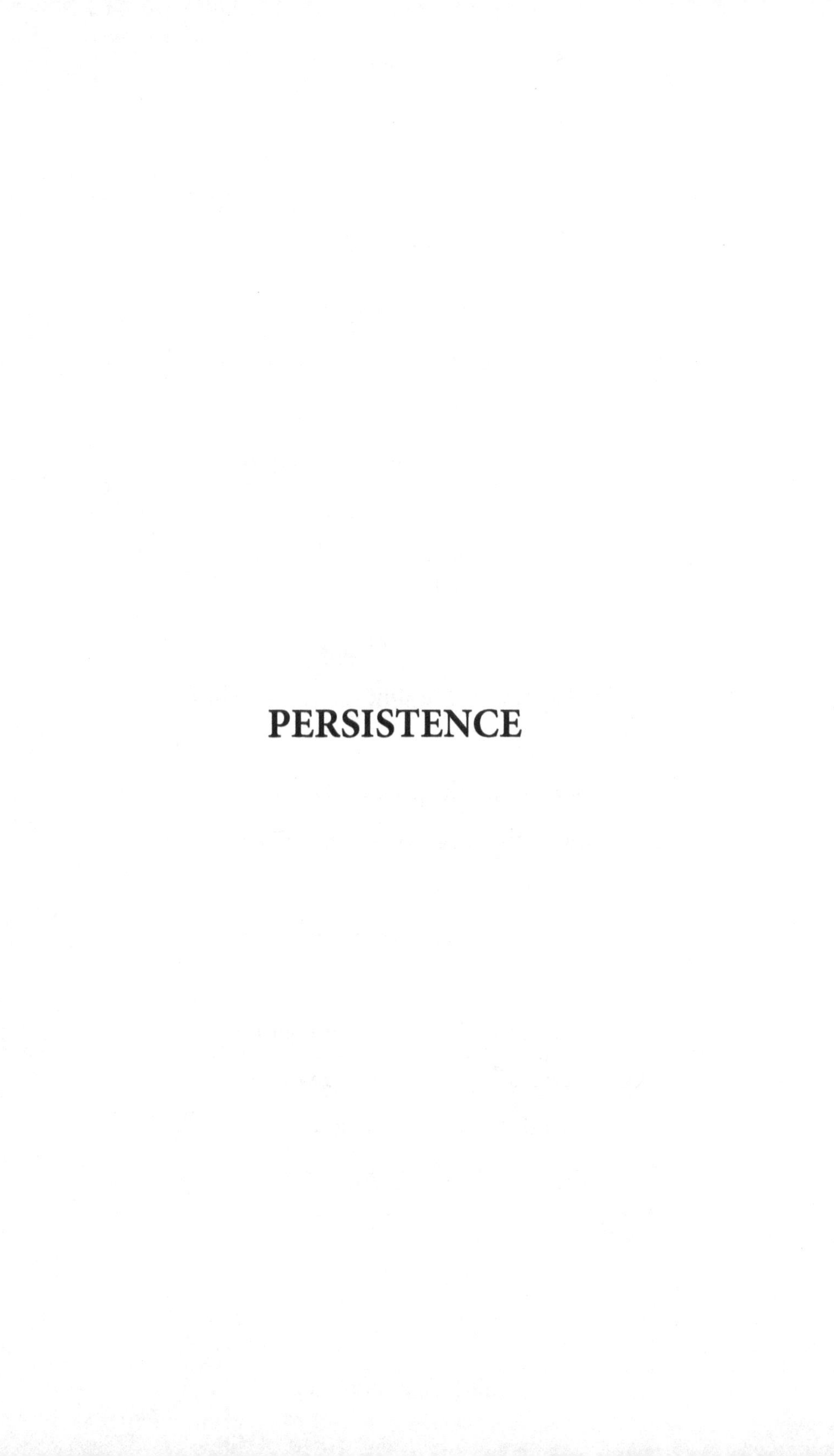

PERSISTENCE

Dream

What's a dream?
Looks like a smooth cream
Filled up to the brim
But for which we must scream.

What's the price of this thing?
To sadden loved beings
Be a bad being
Or sacrifice your health, for the time being.

Sometimes the price looks too much
So much that, it surpasses our inner budget
But still to hold that dream
Is everyone's dream.

In the end, after giving your best
Don't forget, either you will get it
And if not, then make a promise
You will never regret it.

One or Many

I moved away from home
To become someone great
But now I am struggling, even to remain afloat
Isn't it like Titanic? the boat?

Some of us have gone high
And seeing them is quite a sight
Most of them keep a strict diet
And they are called STARS
Like they rule the nights.

Night is dark and space is vast
And it swallows the rest of us
Like it is gobbling after a long fast
And we simply are dissolved
Or blurred in the pages of the past.

Coming back to bed, before the journey ends
Who to blame, what to set on flame
Remains the only aim.
Whether my efforts were worth a penny?
If you will go this path…
Welcome to the world of Many!

New

Every day we want something new
There are many experiences, we can sew
Then why be stuck with some old few?

Ok, let's try something new,
But with the thought
A feeling of failure grew
Is this how we wanna move?
With "What ifs" and "Self-Doubt" as crew.

Who will give us the answer?
We already know that answer
Let's not ignore the voice of the heart
And if you can't listen,
Don't jump to google but be silent for some part.

Will hear the voice
Just lower the noise
Not gonna give up
Will do the new
Even if you call me crazy!

Hello, Hello! Here, Here!

You are reading here,
But your mind is somewhere
Maybe pondering, How's the atmosphere?
Full of gas and sphere
See so fast it moves,
Nothing even near, to compare
I am still talking about your mind
Hello! Hello! Here! Here!

It's such a fast horse
But making it stand
Gives you a magic wand
But no one wants to follow this trend
As it takes effort and skill
To hold this smooth sand
Hello! Hello! Here! Here!

This is a trending duel
Attention seekers want more and more
Giver says sorry it's already two seconds
Please ask no more!

Stagnant

Life seems utterly slow,
Like no there is no flow
Slow enough to make me go low
Feels like a major blow.

Tired of social media,
Missing the Expedia
Present in India,
Still nowhere in Wikipedia.

The poem rhymes
But brings no dime
Like my life moving fine
But I want to shine

I feel stuck
Have no luck
Want to make a buck
Like Mark Zuckerberg.

Ego

Ego starts to develop
As you progress and grow up
As the days of struggle are over
You only wish to cuddle all over.

So, is it wrong to enjoy the fruits?
After one has been through many routes
Don't they deserve a right to power
Yes, but power is given to empower
Not to take bath in a lofty shower.

It feels like
The struggle went very deep
Corroded the very fibre
Which you wanted to uphold and keep
After the event which made you weep.

After facing all season of challenges
One should enjoy and rest
But must keep a check
Is the ego good
To make the ending perfect?

Digital Scar

Walking down the trodden path
After the week went very fast
Was so much wrapped in the virtual world
I can feel the digital scar.

So the feel of dust
Became the needed lust
I tried to book the cab
And lust conspired with fate
And I had to walk the path without a mate.

Halfway through the journey
Now I feel my flesh
Moon was wearing a shiny one piece
Cars were thrusting the dust, geez!

Then someone flashed the beam
Out of the dark, comes an unexpected scene
A girl was tasting her boyfriend's lips
A dog was staring, in search of chubby meat.

Finally came a diversion
That was the needed aversion
From daily immersion
As I walked in dark to my mansion.

Migration

I felt a sudden pull
For the hometown after I got full,
Completed the study
Learnt or not but earned the degree.

So what's the next thing?
Before my next wink
I went to my social feed
Looked at other's achievements
Developed the greed.

Now you know what's next!
You feed the greed and its expectation increased
Fancy homes, fast cars with vacations very far
Now comes the feeling of something missing
Some get that in a bar, some in their fast car.

Birds also migrate
For food or to breed
But they do come back
So they don't have to seek
The healing place when you feel sick.

Like Everyone Else

Lying in the bed every night
I want to give up the fight
But will that be right?
Once I have drawn all the sight.

Someone said, and if not then I made
Better to be crazy, than a lazy
Better to be late than only await
Else who will you be
Eating, talking and sleeping puppet?

There is a whiff of rebellion
Attached to the idea
But who will you be?
If you didn't know the taste of medallion.

Till when will you see others?
What's so special about their leather
Why don't you focus on your feather?
Ok ok I am not your mother
But doesn't this thought bother?
Who will you be? Just like someone another?

Extinguished

There is coldness
Gripping many hearts
Their fire had extinguished
Interest has fallen apart.

What's with the ferocity?
We were supposed to have curiosity
Responsibility to increase prosperity
Here we are, feeling trapped
In a jammed polluted city.

Living life inside walls of matchboxes
Watching life on a small digital screen
Attention, recall and focus are gone
But our aspiration has only grown
For bigger name, fame and home…

It's never late
To own up to your fate
But for that, first, be awake
Realize the current state
You are in prison
With Invisible bar and scared pigeon.

Unwinding

I was hanging there
Where people were unaware,
Nobody was giving a damn care
Everyone was enjoying their own share.

My legs were hurting
Heart was racing
I want to give up on the night
But then someone played
Where's the party tonight!

Amidst the noise and flickering lights
The mind started to feel light
So I closed my eyes and had an insight.

Under the starry sky,
Around the snowy high,
Inside a wooden home
We were dancing, like a kite
Where the music was wind
And the threads were intertwined
As the winds slowly stopped
I was back, where I had rocked
Yet you were still far

So I asked the person at the bar

How do you give peace?

To people who have faced a war…

Deviation

Seeing so much fraud
I wished to go abroad
But will it give me peace?
Home is still an integral piece.

Hopes were many,
Did I finish any?
How to regain the faith?
After you have cheated in math.

What was that fire – Desire
What to get the mission – Passion
Who has the big mouth – Youth
So what's the point of knowledge
Just let things be and don't acknowledge?

When will the slumber end?
After being crazy rich,
Or being in beggar's clan.

Dreams were mine
Thinking about them
Used to make my eyes shine
Now I say I am fine

Attend to fine dine
Am I hiding my spine?
As I am dependent on others
To give me my dreamy feathers
Instead of burning like a sun
Forging my path and having fun.

Monday Blues

Sunday is past
Monday is not moving fast
Everyone must explore
Do they want to chill more?
Or they don't want to work anymore!

Fear of Monday blues
Brings tough Sunday for a few,
I saw many were buying stuff
Standing in a queue,
While some were preparing by
Drinking Mountain Dew!

Let's see the reason
In technical pedia
The reason for this feeling
Is Lord Inertia!

So what's the solution
To this mania?
Increase the speed of life
Doing things you like,
Or decrease the mass
Not by time pass

But by doing something new

And that too fast

Something different from the past!

After Monday

So was Monday really slow?
Or the tension of tomorrow
Was futile and hollow?
Think wisely, cause likewise
Life will follow!

Fear of tomorrow
Thought of yesterday's sorrow
I am so poor, I have to borrow…
Are now very common to mind
Like somebody has put it on rewind.

Isn't life like a wind?
Source and destination unknown
Yet moving along
Like it has to go very long.

Sometimes hot, sometimes cold
However it is, you can't hold
The moments of life
Is like the passing of wind
Light, quick and no visible end.

So let's not waste any time

To see the invisible,

Live in the present

As that's inevitable.

Growth

After a long day
I had nothing left to say
I just wanna lay
But it wants to play.

This "I" and "It" are part of me
What's the difference, let's see.

I want comfort
I want food
I want sleep
I is popular, but only till neighbourhood.

It wants to work
It wants to achieve
It wants to play
It is unpopular but sees beyond the hood.

None of them wants to steal the show
But they are teaching you
Life is precious
Don't let it go
But grow!

Settled or Trapped

Were there some nights

Where sleep doesn't kiss you good night?

At first, you feel, it must be due to some tension

But one day you realise,

This tension will last beyond your pension

So better confront it, without any apprehension.

You were a child with a set routine,

Stories of discipline, Fear of ghosts

Playing till clothes were dirty and nosy face

That was your "base".

"Pillars" are straight and you were thrown into the race

Run! Run! Run! Increase your pace!!!

Be it boards or fancy dress, you have to ace.

Then comes the "ceiling"

Where you tasted the high

And developed first feelings

With such a lovely view from the top,

The world was under your nose.

And then you had the "house"

And this feeling of suffocation started to arouse,

Cause now there is no next

And you are getting questions

Out of context, lying in bed, thinking of unknown mistakes

And heart shouts let me fly out of this Nest…

Spark

Surrounded by the abundance
Food to cater to the buds
Home to relax the bones
Money to fulfil the wish
Love to share all of this.

Then why does the heart feel
There is still one missing fish
In the ocean of life
And that feeling never ceases to exist.

This feeling separates us
From the person we are
And the person we want to be
We wished both to be the same
Yet both share nothing
But just the Name.

So what's the conclusion?
Is it because we are Lazy or Slow?
Or our wish to be some
Is it nothing but a big hoax?
Or we don't know who we are?

Whatever the case

Will run and chase

Cause of the absence

Of that spark in the face.

Young Man

Walking down an old Street
For the exercise of feet
But who knew,
Many emotions were waiting
To meet and greet.

Façade of buildings
Were like abandoned homes,
The mind got curious
How can one spend a single night.
Under this unfortunate plight?

Across the road
A boy was running
Barefooted and smiling,
That made me stop
As earlier, I also used to hop
Across the village, like it's my own shop.

The emotions were deep
I was unable to digest
So wanted to go to sleep
But then in a dream, they shouted
Learn to expand your horizon and face this game
It's just a part of growing, young man!

Lost Among Most

After the noisy day
Before the hopeful dawn
I dance to a song, unknown
Music keeps changing
As I don't control my thoughts.

I want to listen to one particular
But I remember nothing
I feel I am not fine
I scolded my brain
For being so little
But knew the culprit
Is a fickle owner.

Stuck at intersections
Between parallel songs
Intensity keeps changing
From source unknown.

Up and Up

In the walk of life
A need aroused
To end the strife
And get away from the hive.

I searched for the flashlight
In the dark night
To put an end to my daily fight
Which I was doing in broad daylight.

Finally, the sun rises in the east
Which silenced the unrest
Threw me to the crest
And I landed among the best.

Future will make bonds
Between us who were once unknown
Now embrace the change from here on
And it's time to move on and on.

INNOCENCE

Beauty

What is beauty?
A question of curiosity
A body with no deformity
Mind full of creativity
Bond that gives a sense of unity
Or a hug from the one, for whom you are crazy.

The list may never go empty
As infinite moments, stories and views
Work hard to sign up themselves
On the website of beauty.

But why is there a race?
Or craving for association with beauty
Because it separates you out?
But I heard no one wants to die alone.

So what's the solution? Or confusion?
No one really knows
Yet everyone wants to own it
Like it's a piece of telephone.

Fly

I was way above
From the people who are shy
Closed in a box
Where the mosquito is on the fly.

The sight was rare
Left me bizarre
As it was new to know
Mosquitoes can row
Their pedals around numbered rows.

The background was white
Outside view was of afternoon delight
As there was light inside
It shone like a Diamond in a mine
Only with colours of opposite sign.

Nobody cared about my excitement
But I wanted to make an announcement
We should share what holds our attention
Take benefit of this worldly connection.

Hymn

There is a hymn
Which used to run in my dreams
Whose presence gives me a chill
Makes me numb and still.

In the calmness of the night
The coolness of the breeze
Isolation from the mass
That hymn makes a pass
Through the withered trees of my past.

It feels so subtle
Even thought of feeling it
Causes hustle.

That hymn holds magical spell
Designed only for unseen cells
Passes through Outer Layer
Better remains rare.

Holiday

Enough with the philosophy
Let's imagine something rosy
Where relatives are less nosy
Life is cosy.

I woke up and didn't see the clock
The room was cold, dark and locked
Furry blanket slides to the side
With vanilla fragrance, I was back to life.

Time was unknown but hunger has grown
The feast was ready, waiting for me to get busy
Oh the delicacies do increase the fat
But who cares, I will go next for the sunbath.

Lying on the shore, what's more?
Well, I don't want to even think what's more
I am tired of thinking
Have to go for a massage and then explore.

With sips of gossip
Ended the evening
To spend the night
Under the moonlight
With someone special
By my side.

Spring

Winter is gone, spring is on
With the departure of foggy dawn
Arrival of blooming lawn
I feel one with my own
As I walk alone
Leaving my phone
At my lovely home.

I saw children pedalling their way
With chubby cheeks and shining ray
Over the bridge of a flowing river
Where the wind got cold
And cuckoos got the fever
Fireflies were closing their shop
As the fiery sun was about to pop up.

I increased my pace
And dipped my face
In the clear water
Which felt warm
Where fishes whispered in my ear
This is your home
Welcome again, Dear!

Procrastination

After the class, where you don't have to pass
Just have to bend and twist for up to 15 breaths,
Have to keep telling, this too shall pass.
Body was crying, as I walked back
Street food was calling until I crossed the gate.

Plan was to lie down and rest
But then, a thought came
Let's cook some cuisine
Full of spice and create some unrest
Ah but later, I ordered and slept.

A thought in a dream seems abstract
But slowly it revealed and became perfect.

Why do we delay discussing the main subject?
Why didn't you just run and get that object?
Why are the submissions in a race with deadlines?
Why everybody is waiting till Sunday evening
For grocery shopping, or remembering
The weekend passed without any thrill.

The answer was simple: Options.
When time gives you chance, you dance

And procrastinate everything.

So that you can have the option

Option of choosing and taking zero action

So that you feel, you are in control

But only till you are left with no option

But on caffeine to let you do the pending action

And later boast of your pseudo perfection.

Closer

Let's explore the other world
The one that exists
Before Birth, After Death
But how to know
In today's date?
Let's observe the ones
Closer to their birth/death date.
What's the similarity?
Between Toddler and Older
They both uplift, by sharing their gifts.

Toddler stretches our lips
Acts cutely and does random flips
But for all he does for every being
Doesn't want in return, a single thing.

Older ones have giant shoulders
As they carry the huge past, and
Are much closer to the other vast
So they share their knowledge
With anyone who ask!

So what's the gist?

Help and Share

Without expectation of any fare

That's the rhyme coming from the other side

Which seems to be full of mysterious noble minds.

Inner Guide

When the going gets tough
When the future seems rough
When the brain says, enough.

When the urge is to take a puff
When the mind loses fear of cuffs
When you have faced serial bluffs.

Someone is holding the door
Asking you to be indoor
Hold your inner roar and urge to fight
Like a matador.

That someone is your compass
Something to hold on to
If that is lost
Get ready for Holocaust.

Crazy Ones

Feeling of satisfaction
Doesn't come from perfection
But from consistent action
In right direction.

With continuous effort
Thoughts will convert
Into meaningful and tangible work
Irrespective of the fact
You are an introvert or extrovert.

It's easy to commit
Tough to keep
Tougher to absorb the heat
Toughest to do it on repeat.

So, who still wants to settle for less?
Ones who are in the race to impress
Or just want to save their face
Else it would be a matter of disgrace.

But the crazy ones
Want to finish the race
Only to ask
What's next?

Sunday

Clik Clak of clock

Lub Dub of heart

Sii Suu of breath

Pee Poo of horn.

The tingling in the stomach

The strain in the eyes

The tired spine

Heavy mind.

Remorse for past

Anxiety for future

The feeling of the bed

The willingness to stay awake.

I avoid wasting

This time of rest

This day is the best

Sunday – you are always the most welcome guest!

Holi

It's the day
No one should be away
Whoever comes in the way
Paint them, so that they forget their way
And start to play.

It's the day
To let the barriers go away
Between you and the fun
That's waiting in
Sweets, colour and dance in the rain
So go for it, without any delay.

Stop caring for a day
What will they say?
The colours are vivid
And they ask you to play

For those who are mature
For those who are tight
Just close your sight
And remember that child
Smiling under the face
Covered with red, black and white
It's time you unleash that light.

All at Once

I felt it just
Life is so unjust
Always pushing me to adjust
I don't have any trust.

Next moment
I feel innocent
The feeling was magnificent
Like I am a part of it from ancient.

Some other time
I am making bitching rhyme
Full on gossip mode
Ending the mood
Like a hot rod
There is so much variation
In a mood of mine
If life is so different and moody
How can I see it all at one time?

Assume you are standing
In front of little cute round mirrors
Go close and you see a different part of yours
Get a little far, there is only one.

A Meaningful Race

Standing under the tree shade
Surrounded by sun rays
As the railway crossing was closed
And the journey has paused.

I saw an old person
In the lovely bullock cart
With a pointy moustache.

Then a teenager went by
In a fast electric bike
With hairstyle like sharp edge spike.

Oldie noticed the teen
Remembered his days
When he used to run
Faster than a bull, longer than a marathon.

Now the blood has turned into petrol
Muscles are replaced by iron
Money is the soul.

I rested well in the shade
Enjoyed my silent lessons

And noted, before the memory fades

So let's cross the crossing

And start a meaningful race.

Power, Fame, Game

In the food chain
Every animal thinks
He is at the top
He is the point
Where the world should stop.

He can rule the chain
He feels no pain
In killing animals
Lower in the game.

But then why doesn't
Everyone get equal fame?
Why the lion
Stole the fame?

All were attached to their name.
They forgot
Name is never bigger than the game
The one who understood it
Only got the power to tame.

Lockdown

Remember the smile
No! no!
Just remember that smile
That we have lost
In such a short while.

Life turned grey
But yesterday only
We were shouting yay!
That we are the most advanced ones
Can't be anyone's prey.

Now it's time to pray
By standing six feet away
The demand of time asked us to stay
Else be ready to be one with the clay.

All the pride is gone
The illusion is broken
That we are invincible
When nature comes to its might
No one is visible even in broad daylight.

Change

Under the vast dark sky,
Surrounded by nocturnal sounds
With the fragrance of night blooming jasmine
Wrapped under the gentle breeze
With the aftertaste of cheese.

Children were tucked in
Couples were snuggled in
Elders were trying to sleep
When the dogs were ruling the street.

Looking at the distant tree
Brought memories of childhood
When the mind was free
And all it used to think
How to climb that tree.

Walking down the terrace
Up & Down, Side & Straight
Helped me to reduce the growing frown
That world is going to drown
But are we really gonna give up?
Give up our best crown.

Simple Life

It was always there
So why do you see it now?
Because now I feel aware
Ok, So what's in there?

There is a family
Full of squirrels, sparrows and butterflies
Jumping on ground and pine
Running behind each other
Making quirky sound
Which lifted the mind
And gave me a taste of nature divine.

In the distant corner
Was a baby calf
Holding its innocent eyes
Frightened by my first sight, like
I am some monstrous giant

Flowers started to bloom
And asked me, don't you have any work?
Everyone is busy here
I said, looking at you all so busy
Life now feels simple and easy…

Guru

I had given up

As nothing new has been showing up

I prayed to the guru

To please get me through

Give me something, fast and free

He gave me not one but three.

Mountains trying to touch the sky

Inspiring others to stand high

Steep enough to make the weaker cry

So practice hard work

And then nature will comply.

Look at the giant trees

Standing tall, wide and green

Enjoying the wind, dancing with its wings

Holding patience at the age of ninety-three

Knowing one day it will be liberated free.

In the last, oceans are vast

Look at their depth, they hold under

That comes only from surrender

In the end, you will also realize

Surrendering is the only premise.

Inner Peace

Living on the land

Eating from the land

Dying for the land

Do you know in life, where you want to land?

If not, ask your nose to follow the inner smell

Quenching thirst from water

Washing toxins from water

Do you know where to get a true master?

If not, ask your tongue to taste the inner well.

Getting warmth from the fire

Generating energy from the fire

Surrendering at last to the fire

Do you know the root cause of desire?

If not, ask your eyes to look for the controlling wire,

Breathing due to air

Moving due to air

Life is in motion, thanks to air

Do you know how to never despair?

If not, ask your skin to feel the inner atmosphere

Yearning for more space

Ignore the given space

Forgetting the true nature of space

Do you know how to bring a glow to your face?

If not, ask your ears to listen to the inner race.

New City

Moving to a bigger city
Or saying goodbye to Ms. Pretty
Gives an unsettling feeling
Like something is fleeing.

Looking at new faces
Searching for older ones
Starting to fear
Will these people judge
Even on, what I will wear?

Facing new situations
Handling ugly accusations
Unaware of many things
Slow start to appreciate
Small little things.

With all this unease
You always have someone
Whom you want to please.
But during the journey
Don't forget to live
And if you do
Find some time to
Breathe out and release.

ESSENCE

Warmth of Embrace

I was unknown
You made me your own
Faced all the wrong
To comfort my bones.

I was born
And you swore
To shower the love
In the midst of all the thorn.

I tried to lift
To see the goddess
Who has given me this gift,
And you blessed me
With forever bliss.

From cradle to grave
I will be brave
Coz the power I have
That you gave
Just from your embrace.

Butterflies

My heart fluttered
As an imagination occurred
I felt a feeling
Love like
Sweet, simple and appealing.

Facing the window
Towards the passing fields
As she was watching
My sunset cheeks.

Only my eyes were away
With every breath
I wished her attention to stay
Towards my way!

As her aura
Under the hue of sunset
Encompassed the beauty of
Every flora and fauna
We shared a moment
Of content and bliss
Just the way
Sunset feels…

Desire

All you need is a Window
To see the vastness
Not of outside
But the limit of your own.

In the brightness of air,
In the resistance of sunlight
In midst of the warmth of people
And an innocent pounding heart
I saw you.

Your fragrance calls for desire
And beauty spreads the fire
In the midst of so much satire
I only have the pen in your admire

Turbulence brought me back
To the real world
Where I don't know
Will I be able to call you my own?

Some roles will be played by phone
Else I will still be unknown
So be a liar or true to your desire,
Get her number and burn the fire.

Divine

She was the best
Doesn't mean I had a chance
I was like all the rest
Even if I give my best.

Her face is a cheesecake
Smile like fresh dew
On lotus in winter's break.

Her posture can cause fracture
Her ignorance can turn one into
Non performing debenture.

Her fragrance beats the experience
Of all the first glances in her absence
Her walk makes you go crazy
As she is not easy.

If you are sold
That she is gold
You may term yourself
Old.

Cause I saw her in a spree
As she acted like an elegant tree
And then ran to just be free
Like a hippie – carefree.

She is more than what meets the eye
More random than the thoughts that occupy
Cause she is in a spree
Where she lives free.

Connecting Eyes

The beauty of your eyes
Surpasses the depth of sky,
Craving for oneness
Fetches our being
Whom we mostly keep aside.

I was lost in your eyes
Unaware of anything beside,
I wanted to hug
Be your forever bug.

I was peeking
You were staring
I was leaving
You were standing.

Time decided my fate
As I move ahead
But it also gave us an opportunity
To throw the hand
Be wife and husband.

I realized
The last call and
Sprinted to make us whole.

Bonding

Friction will be there
To show its presence
Yet we will sail away
Without it on our way.

We crossed acquaintances behind
Catching friendship
Sharing moments in crime.

Your company is a ripple
That neither pulls
Nor pushes away.

Your charm
is like a perfume
that can give complex
to my every ex.

After all the ups and down
we are still one
connected by such a bond
which everyone craves to hold
Very tough to mould.

Love Story

I tried to gather my senses
To recollect your fragrances
In your absence
To feel your presence.

Our moment was gone
I am here, left alone
But the love you had shown
Is still young in my bones.

I searched for your fingers
Where my thoughts linger
For holding our hearts together
A bit longer.

Your whispers were a sensation
Now your silence is a lullaby
Telling only one story
Glory of our love story.

Sassenach

Different shades of rays
Falling like smooth waves
On slippery caves
That were calm and brave.

First was glance
That was causing my trance
As you laid the hook
With an innocent look.

By turning aside
You shone like full bright
Like a Delhiite.

I became cautious
With wide space
Gorging my face
Sharing her infinite space.

Last was ignorance
To show romance
I love her style
Cause she made me smile.

Poem of the Poet

You shared your heart
It became my favourite art
I will keep hold of it
Even if we are apart.

It holds the curves
Full of colours
Freshness of a flower
Like a blissful shower.

I was mesmerized
Like the whole universe
Flashed before my eyes.

You call me poet
Yet I am only the words
You are the feeling
That gives meaning to my different worlds.

Meaningful Conversation

After a long time
Or for the first time
In a misty morning
Happened to be
My lucky time.

I was a listener
I was a spectator
I was the receiver
Of wisdom
That is needed by many
Packed in conversation
Of two sweet grannies.

Words of praise
Happiness in voice
Warmth in heart
Tears in eyes
Was the companion
Of their conversation
Where we mostly do noise!

They counted their blessings
Thanked the god
For their long innings
Where we are busy winning!

It was short and sweet
I got the gist
Distance between us might be large
So what?
Why to keep our hearts apart?
Good conversation is like rare piece of art.

Waiting for Love

I have always been so good
People love me more than food
I spread smiles in my neighbourhood
Then why don't I get
A life partner who matches my mood.

I feel like I am old
Not fit for flings
I am not that bold.

I thought life is simple
I like to help people
Who don't get it
Before they get wrinkles.

I get it all
Have done yoga & meditation
Under sacred hall
But sometimes I wonder
Is something wrong?
Or am I afraid to accept
My true feelings or nature
Like hiding in a black hole.

Innocent Fool

She already had the feeling
But she needed some excuse
How can she make it easy?
She wants to first test
Am I enough crazy?

I was the fool
Who had no idea of the rule
That either you take the lead
Or get ready to be a passing post
On her crowded feed.

She gave many clues
To start the magic blues
But I was dumb then
Who thought
It might be a very bold move?

For long I felt bad
But now it's all gone
I feel happy
And somewhat grown.

My Comfort Space

Your words are the blanket
For my cold heart
Your sight gives me fire
In the crowd of people
With dirty desire.

Your arms give me support
When I am losing in every sport
Your hug dissolves each issue
In absence of you
I am only left with wet tissue.

Your smile gives the feeling
Of contentment and healing
Your steady walk towards me
Gives new hope, a strong rope.

Your presence lifts the soul
Your touch fulfils every goal
I feel lucky and privileged
Looking at your face
As it is the symbol of
Peaceful and much needed space.

Inspiration

In the race of moving ahead
We have used only our head
Worked hard and relied on fate
Forget love, even memories fade.

But once you are alone
After earning your own lawn
Were the sacrifices
Worth the pawn?

I remember the evening
Sparrows were singing
Phones weren't existing
Under the lantern light
We used to read till night
With dreams of future bright.

Now in the brightness
We feel blindness.

Deficiency created aspirations
Perspired & achieved ambitions
So why is there still an inhibition?
Even after people see me as an Inspiration.

Blackouts

That look reignited the fire
Which I had once blocked
By killing the deepest desire.

Once I was mad
For the connecting,
I wished we had.

I used to tremble
With excitement
From the sounds
Of your heart's rumble.

Reality seeps in
Like water from ceiling
Too small but big enough
To demolish the intact wall.

Will retry to put it out
Might have to vent out
As in life
There is little scope for
Frequent blackouts.

Dissolved Away

You are a dream
That I can never get
So, I find it easier
To simply forget.

Yes, I am a coward now
But I was also brave once
That got me nowhere
So better now
To simply not care.

What will few tears do?
Eventually time will
Dissolve it too.

Break Up

So much sorrow
Encapsulating my light
Like the Sun is covered
When not in sight.

I am in my night
Breathing through darkness
Unaware of the time
Waiting for the dawn
To say
Now it's your time.

But this wait
Where all bad thoughts await
Where uncertainty keeps you awake
Puts so much weight
You want to give up
And curse the fate.

In that numbness
When nothing seems right
Just hang in the fight
The night is only bringing you
Closer to your own light.

Meri Gully Mein

Girl from the valley
Visited my alley,
Wearing her innocent smile
In a long blue dress
Little smaller than Nile.

Wandering eyes
Twitching fingers
Slow and muffled voice
Were blocking her style.

Her style has a hallmark
Of the genuine smile
Cuteness personified
And once she speaks
Your tongue will be tied.

But she is here now
In my world
Away from her valley
Will I be able to
Match her level
Even though I am in my alley?

Rust

You are a treasure
Locked under the rocks
Shackled by thoughts
Acting like robots.

You need some pressure
With proper leisure
With little fun
Under the sun.

Once you get
What was
Worth the wait
You will know.

You were always a gem
Was just covered with dust
With the help of time
Realize all the bad moments
Was just a rust!

Rose

After breaking many hearts
She plucked the rose
For the only one
Who always stood close.

Connection of rose
With heart is like
Artist with art, and
Breath with life.

In between red petals
Behind the velvet texture
Under the rosy fragrance
Exist some thorns.

In the desire of moving up,
One who crosses the thorns
Is eligible for the rose
And experiences its beauty
Like it is his own.

www.ingramcontent.com/pod-product-compliance
Lightning Source LLC
Chambersburg PA
CBHW061357160726
47995CB00001B/361